Vegan Cookbook: 101 Del
Salad, Main Dish, Breakfa
the Whole Family Will Love!

by **Vesela Tabakova**
Text copyright(c)2015 Vesela Tabakova

Table Of Contents

Heart Warming Vegan Meals for all Seasons and Tastes

Our fast-paced lives leave us with less and less time for food planning and preparing healthy meals at home. When you don't have a lot of time to spend on dinner and all you want is to relax with your family, these simple and easy to cook vegan dishes will allow you to get a great meal on the table that the whole family will love in an instant.

As a working mother of teenagers with mixed dietary preferences, I don't have the luxury of long periods in the kitchen and am constantly looking for new nutritious and varied vegan meals to add to my everyday menus. Here's a collection of some of my favorite ridiculously easy vegan recipes that are perfect for a busy weeknight supper or a delicious weekend dinner.

My vegan recipes have been handed down from generation to generation over the years and I have personally tested and tasted them all. They range from crowd-pleasing soup and casseroles, to breakfast and sophisticated desserts. I've also got plenty of vegan kid-friendly recipes, including the best vegan pizza and delicious creamy pasta. All my recipes are simple to prepare and are just the thing to cook when you want a quick weeknight supper or a simple and delicious weekend dinner.

Whether you have made the transition to a vegan lifestyle or you just want to have a few nights in the week without meat, here you'll find plenty of vegan recipes, most of them quick and easy, to inspire you, and please everyone at your table.

Vegan Salads and Appetizers

Spinach and Barley Salad

Serves: 4

Ingredients:

2/3 cup quick-cooking barley

3 cups finely cut spinach leaves

7-8 cherry tomatoes, halved

2-3 green onions, cut

for the dressing:

3 tbsp olive oil

2 tbsp white wine vinegar

1 garlic clove, crushed

salt and black pepper, to taste

Directions:

Cook barley according to package instructions

Whisk the dressing ingredients in a small bowl until smooth. Season with salt and pepper to taste.

Combine barley, spinach, tomatoes and onions in a salad bowl. Drizzle with the dressing, toss to combine and serve.

Roasted Leek and Sweet Potato Salad

Serves: 5

Ingredients:

1 lb sweet potato, unpeeled, cut into 1 inch pieces

3-4 leeks, trimmed and cut into 1 inch slices

a handful of baby spinach leaves

1 cup watercress, rinsed, patted dry and separated from roots

1 tbsp dried mint

2 tbsp olive oil

2 tbsp lemon juice

Directions:

Preheat oven to 350 F. Line a baking tray with baking paper and place the sweet potato and leeks on it. Drizzle with olive oil and sprinkle with mint. Toss to coat. Roast for 20 minutes or until tender.

Place roasted vegetables, baby spinach and watercress in a salad bowl and stir. Sprinkle with lemon juice and serve.

Mediterranean Avocado Salad

Serves: 5

Ingredients:

1 avocado, peeled, halved and cut into cubes

1 cup grape tomatoes

1 cup radishes, sliced

2 tbsp drained capers, rinsed

1 large cucumber, quartered and sliced

a handful of rocket leaves

½ cup green olives, pitted, halved

½ cup black olives, pitted, sliced

7-8 fresh basil leaves, torn

2 tbsp olive oil

2 tbsp red wine vinegar

salt and pepper, to taste

Directions:

Place avocado, cucumber, tomatoes, radishes, rocket, olives, capers and basil in a large salad bowl.

Toss to combine then sprinkle with vinegar and olive oil. Season with salt and pepper, toss again and serve.

Avocado and Cucumber Salad

Serves: 5

Ingredients:

2 avocados, peeled, halved and sliced

2-3 green onions, finely cut

1 cucumber, halved, sliced

1/2 cup cooked sweet corn

for the dressing:

2 tbsp olive oil

3 tbsp lemon juice

1 tbsp Dijon mustard

1/2 cup finely cut dill leaves

salt and pepper, to taste

Directions:

Combine avocado, cucumber, corn and green onions in a deep salad bowl.

Whisk olive oil, lemon juice, dill and mustard until smooth, then drizzle over the salad.

Season with salt and pepper to taste, toss to combine and serve.

Warm Vitamin Salad

Serves: 4

Ingredients:

7 oz cauliflower, cut into florets

7 oz baby Brussels sprouts, trimmed

7 oz broccoli, cut into florets

1/2 cup chopped leeks

for the dressing:

2 tbsp lemon juice

4 tbsp olive oil

1/2 tsp ginger powder

1/2 cup parsley leaves, very finely cut

Directions:

Cook cauliflower, broccoli and Brussels sprouts in a steamer basket over boiling water for 10 minutes or until just tender. Refresh under cold water for a minute and set aside in a deep salad bowl.

Whisk lemon juice, olive oil and ginger powder in a small bowl. Add in salt and pepper to taste; pour over the salad. Top with parsley and serve.

Apple, Walnut and Radicchio Salad

Serves: 4-5

Ingredients:

1 radicchio, trimmed, finely shredded

2 apples, quartered and thinly sliced

a handful of rocket leaves

4-5 green onions, chopped

1/2 cup walnuts, halved and toasted

1 tbsp Dijon mustard

1 tbsp balsamic vinegar

3-4 tbsp olive oil

salt, to taste

Directions:

Prepare the dressing by combining mustard, lemon juice and olive oil.

Place walnuts on a baking tray and bake in a preheated to 400 F oven for 3-4 minutes, or until browned.

Mix radicchio, rocket, apples, onions and walnuts in a large salad bowl. Add the dressing; season with salt, toss to combine and serve.

Apple, Celery and Walnut Salad

Serves: 4

Ingredients:

3 large apples, quartered, cores removed, thinly sliced

1 celery rib, thinly sliced

½ cup walnuts, chopped

1 red onion, thinly sliced

2 tbsp raisins

1/4 cup sunflower seeds

3 tbsp apple cider vinegar

2 tbsp olive oil

salt and black pepper, to taste

Directions:

Mix vinegar, olive oil, salt and pepper in a small bowl. Whisk until well combined.

Place apples, celery, onion, walnuts, raisins and sunflower seeds in a bigger salad bowl. Drizzle with dressing, toss and serve.

Fresh Greens Salad

Serves: 6-7

Ingredients:

1 head red leaf lettuce, rinsed, dried and chopped
1 head green leaf lettuce, rinsed, dried and chopped
1 head endive, rinsed, dried and chopped
1 cup frisee lettuce leaves, rinsed, dried and chopped
3-4 fresh basil leaves, chopped
3-4 fresh mint leaves, chopped
2-3 green onions, chopped
1 tbsp chia seeds
4 tbsp olive oil
3-4 tbsp lemon juice
1 tsp sugar
salt, to taste

Directions:

Place the red and green leaf lettuce, frisee lettuce, endive, onions, basil and mint into a large salad bowl and toss lightly to combine.

Prepare the dressing by whisking lemon juice, olive oil and sugar and pour it over the salad. Sprinkle with chia seeds and season with salt to taste.

Beet Salad with Spinach and Walnuts

Serves: 4

Ingredients:

3 medium beets, steamed and diced

1/2 bag baby spinach leaves

1 red onion, sliced

1/2 cup walnuts, halved and toasted

for the dressing:

1 garlic clove, crushed

2 tbsp lemon juice

3 tbsp olive oil

4-5 fresh mint leaves, chopped

½ tsp salt

Directions:

Place the beats in a steam basket set over a pot of boiling water. Steam for about 12-15 minutes, or until tender. Leave to cool for 5-6 minutes, then peel and dice the beets. Place the spinach leaves in a large salad bowl. Add in the beets, onion and walnuts.

In a smaller bowl, combine the oil, lemon juice, garlic and mint. Whisk and drizzle over the salad.

Beet and Lentil Salad

Serves: 6

Ingredients:

1 can brown lentils, drained and rinsed

1 can pickled beets, drained and cut in cubes

5 oz baby rocket leaves

¼ cup walnuts, toasted and roughly chopped

4-5 green onions, chopped

1 garlic clove, crushed

3 tbsp olive oil

2 tbsp lemon juice

salt and black pepper, to taste

Directions:

Heat olive oil in a frying pan and gently sauté green onions for 1-2 minutes or until softened. Add in garlic and lentils. Cook, for 2 minutes then add in beets and cook for 2-3 minutes more.

Combine baby rocket, walnuts and lentil mixture in a large salad bowl. Sprinkle with lemon juice, toss gently to combine and serve.

Beet and Bean Sprout Salad

Serves: 4-5

Ingredients:

5-6 beet greens, cut in thin strips

2 tomatoes, sliced

1 cup bean sprouts, washed

3 tbsp pumpkin seeds

1 tbsp grated lemon rind

2 garlic cloves, crushed

4 tbsp lemon juice

3 tbsp olive oil

1 tsp salt

Directions:

In a large bowl, toss together beet greens, bean sprouts, tomatoes and pumpkin seeds.

Mix oil and lemon juice with lemon rind, salt and garlic and pour over the salad. Serve chilled.

Roasted Vegetable Salad

Serves: 4

Ingredients:

2 tomatoes, halved

1 medium zucchini, quartered

1 eggplant, ends trimmed, quartered

2 large red pepper, halved, deseeded, cut into strips

2-3 white mushrooms, halved

1 onion, quartered

1 tsp garlic powder

2 tbsp olive oil

for the dressing:

1 tbsp lemon juice

1 tbsp apple cider vinegar

2 tbsp olive oil

1 tsp sumac

5 tbsp crushed walnuts, to serve

Directions:

Whisk olive oil, lemon juice, vinegar and sumac in a bowl.

Preheat oven to 500 F. Place the zucchini, eggplant, peppers, onion, mushrooms and tomatoes on a lined baking sheet.

Sprinkle with olive oil, season with salt, pepper and sumac and roast until golden, about 25 minutes. Divide in 4-5 plates, top with crushed walnuts, drizzle with the dressing and serve.

Light Superfood Salad

Serves: 4

Ingredients:

1 cup mixed green salad leaves

2 cups watercress, rinsed, patted dry and separated from roots

4-5 green onions, chopped

1 avocado, peeled and cubed

10 radishes, sliced

10 green olives, pitted and halved

for the dressing:

1 tbsp lemon juice

2 tbsp apple cider vinegar

2 tbsp olive oil

1 tbsp Dijon mustard

1/2 tsp dried mint

Directions:

Combine all salad ingredients in a large bowl.

In a medium bowl or cup, whisk lemon juice, vinegar, olive oil, mint and mustard until smooth. Pour over salad, toss, and serve.

Baby Spinach Salad

Serves: 4

Ingredients:

1 bag baby spinach, washed and dried

1 red bell pepper, cut in slices

1 cup cherry tomatoes, cut in halves

1 small red onion, finely chopped

1 cup black olives, pitted

for the dressing:

1 tsp dried oregano

1 large garlic clove

3 tbsp red wine vinegar

4 tbsp olive oil

salt and black pepper, to taste

Directions:

Prepare the dressing by blending the garlic and oregano with olive oil and vinegar in a food processor.

Place the spinach leaves in a large salad bowl and toss with the dressing. Add the rest of the ingredients and give everything a toss again. Season to taste with black pepper and salt.

Roasted Pumpkin and Spinach Salad

Serves: 4

Ingredients:

3 cups pumpkin, deseeded, peeled and cut into wedges

1/2 bag baby spinach leaves

1/2 cup canned chickpeas, drained

1/3 cup toasted hazelnuts, coarsely chopped

1 small red onion, thinly sliced

2 tbsp olive oil

2 tbsp maple syrup

for the dressing:

2 tbsp olive oil

2 tbsp lemon juice

1 garlic clove, crushed

Directions:

Preheat oven to 350 F. Line a baking tray with baking paper. Place pumpkin, maple syrup and olive oil in a bowl. Toss to combine. Season with salt and pepper and toss again.

Place pumpkin, in a single layer, on prepared tray. Bake, turning once, for 20-30 minutes or until the pumpkin is tender. Set aside for to cool.

In a small bowl, whisk the dressing ingredients until smooth. Season with salt and pepper to taste.

Place the pumpkin, spinach, chickpeas, onion and hazelnuts in a large salad bowl. Drizzle with the dressing, toss, and serve.

Green Bean and Radicchio Salad with Green Olive Dressing

Serves: 4

Ingredients:

1 lb trimmed green beans, cut to 2-3 inch long pieces

1 radicchio, outer leaves removed, washed, dried

1 small red onion, finely cut

1 cup cherry tomatoes, halved

green olive dressing

1/2 cup green olives, pitted

1/3 cup olive oil

2 garlic cloves, chopped

black pepper and salt, to taste

Directions:

Roughly tear the radicchio leaves and place on a large serving platter.

Steam or boil green beans for about 3-4 minutes until crisp-tender. In a colander, wash with cold water to stop cooking, then pat dry and arrange over the radicchio leaves. Add in red onion and cherry tomatoes.

To make the green olive dressing, place the olives in a food processor and blend until finely chopped. Gradually add the oil and process until a smooth paste is formed. Taste and season with salt and pepper then spoon over salad and serve.

Easy Green Bean Salad

Serves: 6

Ingredients:

2 cups canned green beans, drained

1 small onion, sliced

4 garlic cloves, crushed

3-4 fresh mint leaves, chopped

a bunch of fresh dill, finely chopped

3 tbsp olive oil

1 tbsp apple cider vinegar

salt and pepper, to taste

Directions:

Put the green beans in a medium bowl and mix with onion, mint and dill.

In a smaller bowl, stir olive oil, vinegar, garlic, salt and pepper until smooth. Pour over the green bean mixture and serve.

Three Bean Salad

Serves: 4

Ingredients:

½ cup canned white beans, drained and rinsed

1 lb trimmed green beans, cut to 2 inch long pieces

½ cup canned chickpeas, drained and rinsed

1 red pepper, thinly sliced

1 yellow pepper, thinly sliced

1/2 red onion, thinly sliced

for the dressing:

1 tbsp died basil leaves

2 tbsp olive oil

1 tsp garlic powder

1 tbsp red wine vinegar

salt, to taste

Directions:

Steam green beans for about 3-4 minutes until crisp-tender. Rinse with cold water, pat dry and place in a salad bowl. Mix in the chickpeas, white beans, onions and peppers.

In a small bowl, whisk together vinegar, olive oil, basil and salt. Pour over the salad, toss gently to combine and serve.

Greek Barley Salad

Serves: 4

Ingredients:

2/3 cup quick-cooking barley $210/40$

2-3 green onions, thinly sliced

1 small cucumber, diced

2 green peppers, diced

2 tomatoes, diced

2 tbsp chopped fresh parsley

1 tsp capers, drained and rinsed   — didn't have any

juice of ½ a lemon
                                      30
2 tsp olive oil

1 tsp balsamic vinegar

salt and pepper, to taste

a pinch of dried oregano

Directions:

Cook barley according to package directions.

In a medium bowl, toss together the barley, green onions, cucumber, green peppers, tomatoes, parsley, capers and lemon juice.

In a smaller bowl, stir together the remaining ingredients and pour over the salad. Toss to combine and serve.

5/20

Spring Salad

Serves: 4

Ingredients:

1 green lettuce, washed and drained

1 cucumber, sliced

a bunch of radishes, sliced

a bunch of spring onions, finely cut

juice of half lemon or 2 tbsp of white wine vinegar

3 tbsp olive oil

salt to taste

Directions:

Cut the lettuce into thin strips. Slice the cucumber and the radishes as thinly as possible and chop the spring onions.

Combine all salad ingredients in a large bowl, add the lemon juice and olive oil and season with salt to taste.

Red Cabbage Salad

Serves: 6

Ingredients:

1 small head red cabbage, cored and chopped

1 bunch of fresh dill, finely cut

3 tbsp sunflower oil

3 tbsp red wine vinegar

1 tsp sugar

2 tsp salt

black pepper to taste

Directions:

In a small bowl, mix the oil, red wine vinegar, sugar and black pepper. Place the cabbage in a larger glass bowl. Sprinkle the salt on top and crunch it with your hands to soften.

Pour dressing over the cabbage and toss to coat. Sprinkle with dill, cover it with foil and leave it in the refrigerator for half an hour before serving.

Roasted Peppers with Garlic and Parsley

Serves: 4-6

Ingredients:

2.25 lb red and green bell peppers

3-4 cloves garlic, chopped

½ cup sunflower oil

1/3 cup white wine vinegar

1 cup finely cut fresh parsley

salt and pepper, to taste

Directions:

Grill the peppers or roast them in the oven at 480 F until the skins are a little burnt. Peel the skins and remove the seeds. Cut the peppers into strips lengthwise and layer them in a bowl.

Mix together the oil, vinegar, salt and pepper, chopped garlic and chopped parsley leaves. Pour over the peppers. Cover the roasted peppers and chill for an hour.

Warm Quinoa Salad

Serves: 6

Ingredients:

1 cup quinoa

½ cup green beans, frozen

½ cup sweet corn, frozen

½ cup carrots, diced

½ cup black olives, pitted and halved

2-3 garlic cloves, crushed

2 tbsp fresh dill, finely cut

3 tbsp lemon juice

2 tbsp olive oil

Directions:

Wash quinoa with lots of water. Strain it and cook it according to package directions. When ready, set aside in a large salad bowl and fluff with a fork. Heat olive oil in a large saucepan over medium heat.

Stew green beans, sweet corn, olives and carrots until vegetables are tender. Add this mixture to quinoa and stir to combine.

In a smaller bowl, combine lemon juice, dill and garlic and pour over the warm salad. Add salt and black pepper to taste and serve.

Quinoa and Black Bean Salad

Serves: 6

Ingredients:

1 cup quinoa

1 cup black beans, cooked, rinsed and drained

½ cup sweet corn, cooked

1 red bell pepper, deseeded and chopped

4-5 spring onions, chopped

2 garlic cloves, crushed

1 tbsp dried mint

3 tbsp lemon juice

½ tsp salt

4 tbsp olive oil

Directions:

Rinse quinoa in a fine sieve under cold running water until water runs clear. Put quinoa in a pot with two cups of water. Bring to a boil, then reduce heat, cover and simmer for fifteen minutes or until water is absorbed and quinoa is tender. Fluff quinoa with a fork and set aside to cool.

Put beans, corn, bell pepper, spring onions and garlic in a salad bowl and toss to combine. Add quinoa and toss well again.

In a smaller bowl whisk together lemon juice, salt and olive oil and drizzle over the salad. Toss well and serve.

Roasted Vegetable Quinoa Salad

Serves: 6

Ingredients:

2 zucchinis, peeled and cut into bite sized pieces

1 eggplant, peeled and cut into bite sized pieces

3 roasted red peppers, peeled cut into bite sized pieces

4-5 small white mushrooms, whole

1 cup quinoa

½ cup olive oil

2 tbsp apple cider vinegar

1 tsp summer savory

salt and pepper, to taste

Directions:

Toss the zucchinis, mushrooms and eggplant in half the olive oil, salt and black pepper. Place on a baking sheet in a single layer and bake in a preheated 350 F oven for 30 minutes flipping once.

Wash well, strain, and cook quinoa following package directions.

Prepare the dressing from the remaining olive oil, apple cider vinegar, summer savory, salt and black pepper. In a big bowl combine quinoa, roasted zucchinis, eggplant, mushrooms and roasted red peppers. Toss the dressing into the salad.

Quinoa with Oven Roasted Tomatoes and Pesto

Serves: 6

Ingredients :

1 cup quinoa

2 cups water

1 cup cherry tomatoes, for roasting

½ cup cherry tomatoes, fresh

1 avocado, cut into chunks

½ cup black olives, pitted

for the pesto

2 cloves garlic, chopped

½ tsp salt

½ cup walnuts, toasted

1 cup basil leaves

1 tbsp lemon juice

4-6 tbsp olive oil

1 tsp summer savory

2 tbsp water (optional)

Directions:

Preheat the oven to 350 F and line a baking sheet with foil or baking paper. Wash and dry a cup of cherry tomatoes, arrange them on the baking sheet, drizzle with olive oil and savory and toss to coat well.

Bake the tomatoes for about twenty minutes, flipping once, until they are brown. Sprinkle with salt.

Rinse quinoa very well in a fine mesh strainer under running water; set aside to drain. Place two cups of water and quinoa in a large saucepan over medium-high heat. Bring to the boil, then reduce heat to low. Simmer for fifteen minutes. Set quinoa aside, covered, for ten minutes and fluff with a fork.

Make the homemade pesto by placing garlic, walnuts and ½ teaspoon of salt in a food processor. Add basil and lemon juice and blend in batches until smooth. Add oil, one tablespoon at a time, processing in between, until the pesto is light and creamy. Taste for salt and add more if you like.

In a large mixing bowl, gently mix the quinoa with the tomatoes, avocado and olives. Spoon in the pesto and toss to distribute it evenly.

Cucumber Quinoa Salad

Serves: 6

Ingredients:

1 cup quinoa

2 cups water

1 large cucumber, diced

½ cup black olives, pitted

2 tbsp lemon juice

2 tbsp olive oil

1 bunch fresh dill, finely cut

Directions:

Wash quinoa very well in a fine mesh strainer under running water and set aside to drain. Place quinoa and two cups of cold water in a saucepan over high heat and bring to the boil. Reduce heat to low and simmer for fifteen minutes. Set aside, covered, for ten minutes, then transfer to a large bowl.

Combine quinoa with the finely cut dill, diced cucumber and olives. Prepare a dressing from the lemon juice, olive oil, salt and pepper. Add it to the salad and toss to combine.

Fresh Vegetable Quinoa Salad

Serves: 6

Ingredients:

1 cup quinoa

2 cups water

a bunch of green onions, chopped

2 green peppers, chopped

½ cup black olives, pitted and chopped

2 tomatoes, diced

1 cup sunflower seeds

3 tbsp olive oil

4 tbsp fresh lemon juice

1 tbsp dried mint

Directions:

Prepare the dressing by combining olive oil, lemon juice and dried mint in a small bowl and mixing it well. Place the dressing in the refrigerator until ready to use.

Wash well and cook quinoa according to package directions. When it is ready leave it aside for ten minutes, then transfer it to a large bowl. Add the diced peppers, finely cut green onions, olives and diced tomatoes, toss to combine.

Stir the dressing (it will have separated by this point) and add it to the salad, tossing to coat evenly. Add salt and pepper to taste and sprinkle with sunflower seeds.

Warm Mushroom Quinoa Salad

Serves: 4-5

Ingredients:

1 cup quinoa

2 cups vegetable broth

1 tbsp sunflower oil

2-3 green onions, chopped

2 garlic cloves, chopped

10 white mushrooms, sliced

1-2 springs of fresh rosemary

½ cup sun-dried tomatoes, chopped

2 tbsp olive oil

salt and freshly ground black pepper

½ cup parsley, finely cut

Directions:

Wash well quinoa in plenty of cold water, strain it and put it in a saucepan. Add vegetable broth and bring to the boil. Lower heat and simmer for ten minutes until the broth is absorbed.

Heat oil in a frying pan and sauté onions for 2-3 minutes. Add garlic and sauté for another minute. Add sliced mushrooms and season with salt and pepper. Add the rosemary and cook the mushrooms until soft.

Combine quinoa with mushrooms and sun-dried tomatoes. Serve sprinkled with fresh parsley.

Quinoa Tabbouleh

Serves: 6

Ingredients:

1 cup quinoa

2 cups water

2 cups parsley leaves, finely cut

2 tomatoes, chopped

3 tbsp olive oil

2 garlic cloves, minced

6-7 spring onions, chopped

2-3 tbsp fresh mint leaves, chopped

juice of two lemons

salt and black pepper, to taste

Directions:

Rinse quinoa very well in a fine mesh strainer under running water; set aside to drain. Place water and quinoa in a large saucepan over medium-high heat. Bring to the boil, then reduce heat to low. Simmer for 15 minutes. Set aside, covered, for 10 minutes.

In a large bowl, mix together the finely cut parsley, tomatoes, olive oil, garlic, spring onions and mint. Stir in the already chilled quinoa and season to taste with salt, pepper, and lemon juice.

Quinoa and Asparagus Salad

Serves: 6

Ingredients:

1 cup quinoa

2 cups water

10-11 asparagus stalks, woody ends trimmed, cut

2 bell peppers, deseeded, chopped

¼ cup sunflower seeds

4 spring onions, chopped

2 tbsp fresh parsley, finely cut

2 tbsp lemon juice

1 tsp sugar

2 tbsp olive oil

1 tsp paprika

Directions:

Rinse quinoa very well in a fine mesh strainer under running water; set aside to drain. Place water and quinoa in a large saucepan over medium-high heat. Bring to the boil then reduce heat to low. Simmer for 15 minutes or until just tender. Set aside, covered, for 10 minutes.

Preheat an electric grill or grill pan and cook the asparagus for 2-3 minutes, or until tender crisp. Combine the asparagus, bell pepper, sunflower seeds, spring onions and parsley with the quinoa.

Whisk the lemon juice, sugar, oil and paprika in a small bowl until well combined. Add the dressing to the quinoa mixture. Season with black pepper and toss to combine.

Warm Cauliflower and Quinoa Salad

Serves: 4

Ingredients:

1 small cauliflower, cut into florets

1 cup quinoa

2 cups water

1 tbsp paprika

salt, to taste

½ bunch spring onions, finely cut

5-6 tbsp olive oil

Directions:

Preheat oven to 350 F. Cut the cauliflower into bite sized pieces and place it in a roasting dish. Toss in olive oil, salt and paprika and roast, stirring occasionally until golden on the edges and soft.

Wash quinoa well and place in a medium saucepan with two cups of water. Simmer for 15 minutes then set aside for 3-4 minutes. Serve quinoa topped with cauliflower and sprinkled with spring onions.

Quinoa, Zucchini and Carrot Salad

Serves: 6

Ingredients:

1 cup quinoa

2 cups water

2 big carrots, sliced lengthwise into thin ribbons

1 zucchini, sliced lengthwise into thin ribbons

1 big cucumber, sliced lengthwise into thin ribbons

for the dressing:

2 garlic cloves, minced

2 tbsp orange juice

1 tbsp apple cider vinegar

2 tbsp olive oil

Directions:

Rinse the quinoa very well in a fine mesh strainer under running water; set aside to drain. Place water and quinoa in a large saucepan over medium-high heat. Bring to the boil then reduce heat to low. Simmer for 15 minutes or until just tender. Set aside, covered for 10 minutes.

Peel lengthwise the carrots and zucchini into thin ribbons. Steam them for 3-4 minutes. Peel the cucumber into ribbons too.

Prepare a dressing by mixing the orange juice, vinegar, olive oil and minced garlic.

Serve quinoa on each plate and arrange some of the vegetable stripes over it. Top with 2-3 tablespoons of the dressing.

Vegan Soups

Fresh Asparagus Soup

Serves: 4

Ingredients:

1 lb fresh asparagus, cut into pieces

1 small onion, chopped

3 garlic cloves, chopped

½ cup raw cashews, soaked in warm water for 1 hour

4 cups vegetable broth

2 tbsp olive oil

lemon juice, to taste

Directions:

Sauté onion for 3-4 minutes, stirring. Add in garlic and sauté for a minute more. Add in asparagus and sauté for 3-4 minutes.

Add broth, season with salt and pepper and bring to a boil then reduce heat and simmer for 20 minutes.

Set aside to cool, add cashews, and blend, until smooth. Season with lemon juice and serve.

Creamy Red Lentil Soup

Serves: 4

Ingredients:

1 cup red lentils

1/2 small onion, chopped

1 garlic clove, chopped

1 red pepper, chopped

2 cups water

1 can coconut milk

3 tbsp olive oil

1 tsp paprika

1/2 tsp ginger

salt and black pepper, to taste

Directions:

Heat olive oil in a large saucepan and sauté onion, garlic, red pepper, paprika, ginger and cumin, stirring. Add in red lentils and water. Bring to a boil, cover, and simmer for 20 minutes.

Add in coconut milk and simmer for 5 more minutes. Remove from heat, season with salt and black pepper, and blend until smooth.

Lentil, Barley and Kale Soup

Serves: 4

Ingredients:

2 medium leeks, chopped

2 garlic cloves, chopped

2 bay leaves

1 can tomatoes, diced and undrained

1/2 cup red lentils

1/2 cup barley

1 bunch kale, coarsely chopped

4 cups vegetable broth

3 tbsp olive oil

1 tbsp paprika

½ tsp cumin

Directions:

Heat olive oil in a large saucepan over medium-high heat and sauté leeks and garlic until fragrant. Add in cumin, paprika, tomatoes, lentils, barley and vegetable broth. Season with salt and pepper.

Cover and bring to a boil then reduce heat and simmer for 40 minutes or until barley is tender. Add in kale and let it simmer for a few minutes more until it wilts.

Spinach and Mushrooms Soup

Serves: 4-5

Ingredients:

1 small onion, finely cut

1 small carrot, chopped

1 small zucchini, diced

1 medium potato, diced

6-7 white mushrooms, chopped

2 cups chopped fresh spinach

4 cups vegetable broth or water

4 tbsp olive oil

salt and black pepper, to taste

Directions:

Heat olive oil in a large pot over medium heat. Add potato, onion and mushroom and cook until vegetables are soft but not mushy.

Add chopped fresh spinach, zucchini and vegetable broth and simmer for about 20 minutes. Season to taste with salt and pepper.

Broccoli and Potato Soup

Serves: 4-5

Ingredients:

1 lb broccoli, cut into florets

2 potatoes, chopped

1 onion, chopped

3 garlic cloves, crushed

4 cups water

2 tbsp olive oil

¼ tsp ground nutmeg

Directions:

Heat oil in a large saucepan over medium-high heat. Add onion and garlic and sauté, stirring, for 3 minutes, or until soft.

Add in broccoli, potato and 4 cups of cold water. Cover, bring to a boil, reduce heat and simmer, stirring, for 10-15 minutes, or until potatoes are tender.

Remove from heat and blend until smooth. Return to pan and cook until heated through. Season with nutmeg and black pepper before serving.

Moroccan Lentil Soup

Serves: 7-8

Ingredients:

1 cup red lentils

1 cup canned chickpeas, drained

1 onion, chopped

2 cloves garlic, minced

1 cup canned tomatoes, chopped

1 cup canned white beans, drained

3 carrots, diced

1 celery rib, diced

5 cups water

3 tbsp olive oil

1 tsp ginger, grated

1 tsp ground cardamom

1/2 tsp cumin

Directions:

In a large pot, sauté onions, garlic and ginger in olive oil for about 5 minutes. Add the water, lentils, chickpeas, white beans, tomatoes, carrots, celery, cardamom and cumin.

Bring to a boil for a few minutes, then simmer for half an hour or longer until the lentils are tender. Puree half the soup in a food processor or blender. Return the pureed soup to the pot, stir and serve.

Hearty Italian Minestrone

Serves: 4-5

Ingredients:

¼ head cabbage, chopped

2 carrots, chopped

1 celery rib, thinly sliced

1 small onion, chopped

2 garlic cloves, chopped

1 cup canned tomatoes, diced, undrained

1 cup fresh spinach, torn

1/2 cup pasta, cooked

3 cups water

2 tbsp olive oil

black pepper and salt, to taste

Directions:

Sauté the carrots, cabbage, celery, onion and garlic in oil for 5 minutes in a deep saucepan. Add water and tomatoes and bring to a boil.

Reduce heat and simmer uncovered, for 20 minutes, or until vegetables are tender. Stir in spinach, pasta, and season with pepper and salt to taste.

French Vegetable Soup

Serves: 6

Ingredients:

1 leek, thinly sliced

1 large zucchini, peeled and diced

1 cup green beans, halved

2 garlic cloves, chopped

1 cup canned tomatoes, chopped

3.5 oz vermicelli, broken into small pieces

3 cups vegetable broth

3 tbsp olive oil

black pepper, to taste

Directions:

Sauté the leek, zucchini, green beans and garlic for about 5 minutes, stirring. Add in the vegetable broth and tomatoes and bring to a boil then reduce heat.

Add black pepper to taste and simmer for 10 minutes or until the vegetables are tender but still holding their shape. Stir in the vermicelli. Cover again and simmer for a further 5 minutes. Serve warm.

Beetroot and Carrot Soup

Serves: 5-6

Ingredients:

4 beets, washed and peeled

2 carrots, peeled, chopped

2 potatoes, peeled, chopped

1 small onion, chopped

2 cups vegetable broth

2 cups water

3 tbsp olive oil

1 cup finely cut green onions, to serve

Directions:

Peel and chop the beets. Heat olive oil in a saucepan over medium-high heat and sauté the onion and carrot until tender. Add in beets, potatoes, broth and water. Bring to the boil then reduce heat and simmer, partially covered, for 30 minutes, or until beets are tender. Cool slightly.

Blend soup in batches until smooth. Return it to pan over low heat and cook, stirring, for 4-5 minutes, or until heated through. Season with salt and pepper. Serve sprinkled with green onions.

Celery, Apple and Carrot Soup

Serves: 4

Ingredients:

2 celery ribs, chopped

1 large apple, chopped

1/2 small onion, chopped

3 carrots, chopped

2 garlic cloves, crushed

4 cups vegetable broth

3 tbsp olive oil

1 tsp ginger powder

salt and black pepper, to taste

Directions:

Heat olive oil over medium-high heat and sauté onion, garlic, celery and carrots for 3-4 minutes, stirring. Add in ginger, apple and vegetable broth.

Bring to a boil then reduce heat and simmer, covered, for 10 minutes. Blend until smooth and return to the pot. Cook over medium-high heat until heated through. Season with salt and pepper to taste and serve.

Monastery Style White Bean Soup

Serves: 6-7

Ingredients:

2 cups white beans

2-3 carrots

1 large onion, finely chopped

1-2 tomatoes, grated

1 red bell pepper, chopped

1/2 cup finely cut fresh parsley

1 tbsp dried mint

1 tbsp paprika

¼ cup sunflower oil

salt, to taste

Directions:

Soak the beans in cold water for 3-4 hours or overnight, drain and discard the water.

Cover the beans with cold water. Add in oil, finely chopped carrots, onion and bell pepper.

Bring to a boil and simmer until the beans are tender. Add the grated tomatoes, mint, paprika and salt. Simmer for another 15 minutes. Serve sprinkled with finely chopped parsley.

Creamy Cauliflower Soup

Serves: 6-7

Ingredients:

1 onion, finely cut

1 medium head cauliflower, chopped

2-3 garlic cloves, minced

½ cup raw cashews, soaked in warm water for 1 hour

3 cups vegetable broth

1 cup coconut milk

¼ cup olive oil

salt, to taste

black pepper, to taste

Directions:

Heat the olive oil in a large pot over medium heat and gently sauté the onion, cauliflower and garlic. Stir in the vegetable broth and bring the mixture to a boil.

Reduce heat, cover, and simmer for 30 minutes. Remove the soup from heat, add in cashews, coconut milk, and blend in a blender or with a hand mixer. Season with salt and pepper to taste.

Pumpkin and Bell Pepper Soup

Serves: 4

Ingredients:

1 medium leek, chopped

9 oz pumpkin, peeled, deseeded, cut into small cubes

1/2 red bell pepper, cut into small pieces

1 can tomatoes, undrained, crushed

3 cups vegetable broth

1/2 tsp cumin

salt and black pepper, to taste

Directions:

Heat the olive oil in a medium saucepan and sauté the leek for 4-5 minutes. Add in the pumpkin and bell pepper and cook, stirring, for 5 minutes.

Add tomatoes, broth, and cumin and bring to a boil. Cover, reduce heat to low, and simmer, stirring occasionally, for 30 minutes or until vegetables are soft. Season with salt and pepper and leave aside to cool. Blend in batches and reheat to serve.

Creamy Potato Soup

Serves: 6-7

Ingredients:

4-5 medium potatoes, peeled and diced

2 carrots, chopped

1 zucchini, chopped

1 celery rib, chopped

5 cups water

3 tbsp olive oil

½ tsp dried rosemary

salt and black pepper, to taste

1/2 cup fresh parsley, finely cut

Directions:

Heat olive oil over medium heat and sauté the vegetables for 2-3 minutes. Add 4 cups of water, rosemary and bring the soup to a boil, then lower heat and simmer until all the vegetables are tender.

Blend soup in a blender until smooth. Serve warm, seasoned with black pepper and parsley sprinkled over each serving.

Shredded Cabbage Soup

Serves: 4-5

Ingredients:

1 onion, finely chopped

1 small cabbage, shredded

1 carrot, sliced

1 medium potato, peeled and diced

1 celery rib, sliced

2 tomatoes, diced

3 cups vegetable broth

3 tbsp sunflower oil

1 tsp cumin

salt, to taste

black pepper, to taste

Directions:

Heat sunflower oil over medium heat and gently sauté the onion for 2-3 minutes. Add in cabbage and sauté, stirring, for 2-3 minutes. Add carrots, potatoes, celery, tomatoes and cumin and stir again.

Add vegetable broth and bring the soup to a boil then reduce heat and simmer for 40 minutes. Season with salt and black pepper to taste.

Mediterranean Chickpea Soup

Serves: 7-8

Ingredients:

2 cups canned chickpeas, drained

1 onion, finely cut

2 cloves garlic, crushed

1 cup canned tomatoes, diced

6 cups vegetable broth

3 tbsp olive oil

1 bay leaf

½ tsp crushed rosemary

Directions:

Sauté onion and garlic in olive oil in a heavy soup pot. Add broth, chickpeas, tomato, bay leaf, and rosemary.

Bring to a boil then reduce heat and simmer for 30 minutes.

Wild Mushroom Soup

Serves: 4

Ingredients:

1 lb mixed wild mushrooms

1 onion, chopped

2 garlic cloves, crushed

1 tsp dried thyme

3 cups vegetable broth

3 tbsp olive oil

salt and pepper, to taste

Directions:

Sauté onions and garlic in a large soup pot untill transparent. Add thyme and mushrooms.

Stir and cook for 10 minutes, then add vegetable broth and simmer for another 10-20 minutes. Blend, season and serve.

Spinach Soup

Serves: 4

Ingredients:

14 oz frozen spinach

1 large onion or 4-5 green onions

1 carrot, chopped

1/4 cup white rice

1-2 cloves garlic, cut

3 cups water

3-4 tbsp olive or sunflower oil

1 tsp paprika

black pepper, to taste

salt, to taste

Directions:

Heat oil in a cooking pot. Add the onion and carrot and sauté together for a few minutes, until just softened. Add chopped garlic, paprika and rice and stir for a minute. Remove from heat.

Add the spinach along with about 3 cups of hot water and season with salt and pepper. Bring back to the boil, then reduce the heat and simmer for around 30 minutes.

Tomato and Quinoa Soup

Serves: 4

Ingredients:

4 cups chopped fresh tomatoes or 2 cups canned tomatoes

1 large onion, diced

1/3 cup quinoa, washed very well

3 cups water

2 garlic cloves, minced

3 tbsp olive oil

1 tsp salt

½ tsp black pepper

1 tsp sugar

1 cup finely cut fresh parsley

Directions:

Sauté onions and garlic in olive oil in a large soup pot. When onions have softened, add tomatoes and water and bring to a boil. Lower heat and simmer for 5 minutes.

Blend the soup then return to the pot. Stir in quinoa and sugar and bring to a boil again, then reduce heat and simmer 15 minutes, stirring occasionally. Sprinkle with parsley and serve.

Spinach, Leek and Quinoa Soup

Serves: 4-5

Ingredients:

½ cup quinoa, very well washed

2 leeks halved lengthwise and sliced

1 onion, chopped

2 garlic cloves, chopped

1 can diced tomatoes, (15 oz), undrained

2 cups fresh spinach, cut

4 cups vegetable broth

2 tbsp olive oil

salt and pepper, to taste

Directions:

Heat olive oil in a large pot over medium heat and sauté onion for 2 minutes, stirring. Add leeks and cook for another 2-3 minutes, then add garlic and stir. Season with salt and black pepper to taste.

Add the vegetable broth, canned tomatoes and quinoa. Bring to a boil then reduce heat and simmer for 10 minutes. Stir in spinach and cook for another 5 minutes.

Vegetable Quinoa Soup

Serves: 6

Ingredients:

½ cup quinoa

1/2 onion, chopped

1 potato, diced

1 carrot, diced

1 red bell pepper, chopped

2 tomatoes, chopped

1 small zucchini, peeled and diced

4 cups water

1 tsp dried oregano

3-4 tbsp olive oil

black pepper, to taste

2 tbsp fresh lemon juice

Directions:

Rinse quinoa very well in a fine mesh strainer under running water; set aside to drain.

Heat the oil in a large soup pot and gently sauté the onions and carrot for 2-3 minutes, stirring every now and then. Add in potato, bell pepper, tomatoes, spices and water. Stir to combine.

Cover, bring to a boil, then lower heat and simmer for 10 minutes. Add in the quinoa and the zucchini; cover and simmer for 15 minutes or until the vegetables are tender. Add in the lemon juice; stir to combine and serve.

Vegan Main Dish Recipes

Avocado and Rocket Pasta

Serves: 4

Ingredients:

3 cups cooked small pasta

½ cup cooked sweet corn

1 large avocado, peeled and diced

1 cup baby rocket leaves

5-6 fresh basil leaves, chopped

3 tbsp olive oil

3 tbsp lemon juice

Directions:

Whisk olive oil, lemon juice and basil in a small bowl. Season with salt and pepper to taste.

Combine pasta, avocado, corn and baby rocket. Add oil mixture and toss to combine.

Delicious Broccoli Pasta

Serves: 4

Ingredients:

3 cups cooked small pasta

2 cups broccoli florets, cooked

1/3 cup walnuts, chopped

2 garlic cloves, chopped

10 cherry tomatoes, halved

5-6 fresh basil leaves

3 tbsp olive oil

3 tbsp lemon juice

Directions:

Combine olive oil, lemon juice, garlic, walnuts, basil and broccoli in blender. Season with salt and pepper to taste and blend until smooth.

Combine pasta, broccoli mixture and cherry tomatoes, toss, and serve.

Creamy Butternut Squash Spaghetti

Serves: 4

Ingredients:

12 oz spaghetti

3 cups butternut squash, peeled, cut into small pieces

1/2 small onion, chopped

2 garlic cloves, chopped

1 carrot, cut

1 cup vegetable broth

5-6 fresh sage, chopped

1 tsp paprika

3 tbsp olive oil

salt and black pepper, to taste

Directions:

Heat olive oil in a large skillet and cook the onions, garlic and carrot until soft. Add the paprika and the pumpkin and mix well. Stir in vegetable broth and bring the mixture to a boil, then reduce heat and simmer until pumpkin is soft, about 15 to 20 minutes. Set aside to cool.

In a large pot of boiling salted water, cook spaghetti according to package instructions. Drain and set aside in a large bowl.

Once the pumpkin mixture has cooled, purée it until smooth, then season with salt and pepper to taste.

Combine spaghetti, pumpkin mixture and fresh sage leaves, toss, and serve.

Sweet Potato Spaghetti

Serves: 4

Ingredients:

12 oz spaghetti

1 sweet potato peeled, slice into quarters

1/2 small onion, sliced

2 garlic cloves, chopped

1 carrot, quartered

1 large parsnip, quartered

1 tbsp tomato paste

1 tbsp rosemary, chopped

1/2 tsp thyme

4 tbsp olive oil

1 tbsp balsamic vinegar

salt and black pepper, to taste

1 cup finely gut green onions, to serve

Directions:

Arrange sweet potatoes, onion, carrot and parsnip on a lined baking sheet. Toss it in olive oil, salt, pepper and balsamic vinegar. Roast at 380 F until the vegetables are tender, about 20 minutes.

In a large pot of boiling salted water, cook spaghetti according to package instructions. Drain and set aside in a large bowl.

Once the vegetables have cooled, purée them together with tomato paste, thyme and rosemary. Add some water as needed to get the blade moving.

Combine spaghetti with the sauce. Add spaghetti water as needed to loosen. Sprinkle with chopped green onions and serve.

Quick Orzo and Zucchini Dinner

Serves: 4-5

Ingredients:

1 cup orzo

2-3 medium zucchinis, peeled and cubed

1/2 onion

1/2 cup white wine

3 tbsp olive oil

1 tbsp dried oregano

1/3 cup fresh dill, finely cut

1 tsp salt

1 tsp fresh black pepper

2 tbsp lemon juice

Directions:

Cook the orzo according to package directions (in salted water) and rinse thoroughly with cold water when you strain it. Add in a tbsp of olive oil, stir, and set aside.

Gently sauté onion and zucchinis in 2 tbsp of olive oil, stirring, until onions are translucent. Add oregano and white wine and cook uncovered on low heat for 10 minutes. Add in orzo and stir to combine well. Add lemon juice, dill, and simmer, covered for 5 more minutes.

Best Vegan Pizza

Serves: 4

Ingredients:

1 store-bought or homemade dough

1/3 cup onion, chopped

1 cup mushrooms, chopped

1/2 cup each red and green bell pepper, chopped

1/2 cup tomato sauce

1/2 cup vegan cheese

2 tbsp olive oil

1/2 tsp oregano

1 tsp dried basil

1/2 tsp garlic powder

Directions:

Heat a large skillet on medium heat and sauté the onion and peppers for 4-5 minutes until slightly charred. Add in the mushrooms, garlic powder, oregano and basil and sauté for 5 minutes more. Season with salt and black pepper to taste.

Roll out dough onto a floured surface and transfer to a parchment-lined 12 inch round baking sheet or pizza stone.

Top it with fresh or canned tomato sauce, vegan cheese and the sautéed vegetables.

Bake for 25-30 minutes in a preheated to 450 F oven or until the crust is golden brown and the sauce is bubbly. Let rest for 5 minutes before cutting, then serve immediately.

Eggplant and Chickpea Stew

Serves: 4

Ingredients:

2-3 eggplants, peeled and diced

1 onion, chopped

2-3 garlic cloves, crushed

8 oz can chickpeas, drained

8 oz can tomatoes, undrained, diced

1 tbsp paprika

1/2 tsp cinnamon

1 tsp cumin

3 tbsp olive oil

salt and pepper, to taste

Directions:

Peel and dice the eggplants. Heat olive oil in a large deep frying pan and sauté onions and crushed garlic. Add in paprika, cumin and cinnamon. Stir well to coat evenly. Sauté for 3-4 minutes until the onions have softened.

Add in the eggplant, tomatoes and chickpeas. Bring to a boil, lower heat and simmer, covered, for 15 minutes, or until the eggplant is tender.

Uncover and simmer for a few more minutes until the liquid evaporates.

Green Pea and Mushroom Stew

Serves: 4

Ingredients:

1 cup green peas (fresh or frozen)

4 large mushrooms, sliced

3 green onions, chopped

1-2 cloves garlic

4 tbsp sunflower oil

1/2 cup water

1/2 cup finely chopped dill

salt and black pepper, to taste

Directions:

In a saucepan, sauté mushrooms, green onions and garlic. Add in the green peas and simmer for 10 minutes until tender.

When ready sprinkle with dill and serve.

Tomato Leek Stew

Serves: 5-6

Ingredients:

1 lb leeks, cut into rings

1/2 cup vegetable broth

2 tbsp tomato paste

4 tbsp sunflower oil

1 tbsp dried mint

salt to taste

fresh ground pepper to taste

Directions:

Heat oil in a heavy wide saucepan or sauté pan. Add in leeks, salt, pepper, and sauté, stirring, for 5 minutes. Add in vegetable broth and bring to a boil.

Cover and simmer over low heat, stirring often, for about 10-15 minutes or until leeks are tender. Gently stir in tomato paste and dried mint, raise heat to medium, uncover and simmer for 5 minutes.

Potato and Leek Stew

Serves: 4

Ingredients:

12 oz potatoes, diced

2-3 leeks cut into thick rings

5-6 tbsp olive oil

1 cup water

1/2 cup finely cut parsley

1 tsp paprika

salt and black pepper, to taste

Directions:

Heat olive oil in a heavy wide saucepan or sauté pan. Add in leeks, paprika, salt and pepper, and sauté for 2-3 minutes, stirring. Add in potatoes and water. The water should cover the vegetables.

Bring to a boil and simmer until vegetables are tender. Sprinkle with finely chopped parsley and serve.

Spinach with Rice

Serves: 4

Ingredients:

1.5 lb fresh spinach, washed, drained and chopped

1/2 cup rice

1 onion, chopped

1 carrot, grated

5 tbsp olive oil

2 cups water

Directions:

Heat the oil in a large skillet and cook the onions until soft. Add paprika, carrot and rice and stir. Add two cups of warm water stirring constantly as the rice absorbs it, and simmer for 10 minutes.

Wash the spinach cut it in strips then add to the rice and cook until it wilts. Remove from heat and season to taste.

Rich Vegetable Stew

Serves: 6

Ingredients:

3-4 potatoes, peeled and diced

2 tomatoes, diced

2 carrots, chopped

1 onion, finely chopped

1 zucchini, peeled and cut

1 eggplant, peeled and cut

1 celery rib, chopped

1/2 cup green peas, frozen

1/2 green beans, frozen

3 tbsp sunflower oil

1 bunch of parsley

1 tsp black pepper

1 tsp salt

Directions:

In a deep saucepan, sauté the finely chopped onion, carrots and celery in a little oil. Add in green peas, the green beans, black pepper and stir well. Pour over 1 cup of water, cover and let simmer.

After 15 minutes add the diced potatoes, the zucchini, the eggplant and the tomato.

Transfer everything into an ovenproof baking dish, sprinkle with parsley and bake for about 30 minutes at 350 F.

Hearty Baked Beans

Serves: 8-10

Ingredients:

1 1/2 dried white beans

2 medium onions

1 red bell pepper, chopped

1 carrot, chopped

1/4 cup sunflower oil

1 tsp paprika

1 tsp black pepper

1 tbsp plain flour

½ bunch fresh parsley and mint

1 tsp salt

Directions:

Wash the beans and soak them in water overnight. In the morning discard the water, pour enough cold water to cover the beans, add one of the onions, peeled but left whole. Cook until the beans are soft but not falling apart. If there is too much water left, drain the beans.

Chop the other onion and fry it a frying pan along with the chopped bell pepper and the carrot. Add in paprika, plain flour and the beans.

Stir well and pour the mixture in a baking dish along with some parsley, mint, and salt. Bake in a preheated to 350 F oven for 20 minutes. The beans should not be too dry. Serve warm.

Rice Stuffed Bell Peppers

Serves: 4-5

Ingredients:

8 bell peppers, cored and seeded

11/2 cups rice

2 onions, chopped

1 tomato, chopped

1/2 cup fresh parsley, chopped

3 tbsp olive oil

1 tbsp paprika

Directions:

Heat the olive oil and sauté the onions for 2-3 minutes. Add in paprika, rice, diced tomato and season with salt and pepper. Add ½ cup of hot water and cook the rice, stirring, until the water is absorbed.

Stuff each pepper with rice mixture using a spoon. Every pepper should be ¾ full. Arrange the peppers in a deep ovenproof dish and top up with warm water to half fill the dish.

Cover and bake for about 20 minutes at 350 F. Uncover and cook for another 15 minutes until the peppers are well cooked through.

Bell Peppers Stuffed with Beans

Serves: 5

Ingredients:

10 dried red bell peppers

1 cup dried white beans

1 onion, finely cut

3 cloves garlic, chopped

2 tbsp flour

1 carrot, chopped

1 cup fresh parsley, finely cut

1/2 cup crushed walnuts

1 tsp paprika

salt

Directions:

Put the dried peppers in warm water and leave them for 1 hour.

Cook the beans. Gently sauté onion and carrot and combine with the cooked beans. Add in the finely chopped parsley and walnuts. Stir.

Drain the peppers, then fill them with the bean mixture and arrange in a baking dish, covering the openings with flour to seal them during the baking. Bake for about 30 minutes at 350 F

Stuffed Grapevine Leaves

Serves: 6

Ingredients:

1.5 oz grapevine leaves, canned

2 cups rice

2 onions, chopped

2-3 cloves garlic, chopped

1/2 cup of currants

1/2 cup fresh parsley, finely cut

1/2 cup fresh dill, finely cut

1 lemon, juice only

1 tsp dried mint

1 tsp salt

1 tsp black pepper

6 tbsp virgin olive oil

Directions:

Heat 3 tablespoons of olive oil in a frying pan and sauté the onions and garlic until golden. Add the washed and drained rice, the currants, dill and parsley and sauté, stirring. Add in lemon juice, black pepper, dried mint and salt.

Place a grapevine leaf on a chopping board, with the stalk towards you and the vein side up. Place about 1 teaspoon of the filling in the center of the leaf and towards the bottom edge. Fold the bottom part of the leaf over the filling, then draw the sides in and towards the middle, rolling the leaf up. The vine leaves should be well tucked in, forming a neat parcel. The stuffing should feel compact and evenly distributed.

Cover the bottom of a pot with grapevine leaves and arrange the stuffed vine leaves, packing them tightly together, on top. Pour in some water, to just below the level of the stuffed leaves. Place a small, flat ovenproof plate upside down on top, in order to prevent scattering.

Cover with a lid, bring to a boil, then reduce heat and simmer for about an hour checking occasionally that the bottom of the pot does not burn. Serve warm or cold.

Stuffed Cabbage Leaves

Serves: 8

Ingredients:

20-30 pickled cabbage leaves

1 onion, finely cut

2 leeks, chopped

1 1/2 cup white rice

1/2 cup currants

1/2 cup almonds, blanched, peeled, and chopped

2 tsp paprika

1 tbsp dried mint

1/2 tsp black pepper

½ cup olive oil

salt, to taste

Directions:

Sauté the onion and leeks in olive oil for about 2-3 minutes. Stir in paprika, black pepper and rice and continue sautéing until the rice is translucent. Remove from heat and add the currants, finely chopped almonds and the peppermint. Add salt only if the cabbage leaves are not too salty.

In a large pot, place a few cabbage leaves on the base. Place a cabbage leaf on a large plate with the thickest part closest to you. Spoon 1-2 teaspoons of the rice mixture and fold over each edge to create a tight sausage-like parcel. Place in the pot, making two or three layers.

Cover with a few cabbage leaves and pour over some boiling

water so that the water level remains lower than the top layer of cabbage leaves. Top with a small plate upside down to prevent scattering.

Bring to the boil then lower the heat and cook for around 40 minutes. Serve warm or at room temperature.

Green Bean and Potato Stew

Serves: 5-6

Ingredients:

2 cups green beans, fresh or frozen

2 onions, chopped

3-4 potatoes, peeled and diced

2 carrots, cut

4 cloves garlic, crushed

1 cup fresh parsley, chopped

1/2 cup fresh dill, finely chopped

4 tbsp olive oil

1/2 cup water

2 tsp tomato paste

salt and pepper, to taste

Directions:

Heat olive oil in a deep saucepan and gently sauté the onions and garlic. Add in green beans and the remaining ingredients.

Cover, and simmer over medium heat for about an hour or until all vegetables are tender. Check after 30 minutes; add more water if necessary. Serve sprinkled with fresh dill.

Cabbage and Rice Stew

Serves: 4

Ingredients:

1 cup long grain white rice

2 cups water

2 tbsp olive oil

1 small onion, chopped

1 clove garlic, crushed

1/4 head cabbage, cored and shredded

2 tomatoes, diced

1 tbsp paprika

1/2 cup parsley, finely cut

salt and black pepper, to taste

Directions:

Heat the olive oil in a large pot. Add in onion and garlic and cook until transparent. Add paprika, rice and water, stir, and bring to boil. Simmer for 10 minutes.

Add in cabbage, tomatoes, and cook for about 20 minutes, stirring occasionally, until the cabbage cooks down. Season with salt and pepper and serve sprinkled with parsley.

Rice with Leeks and Olives

Serves: 4-6

Ingredients:

6 large leeks, cleaned and sliced into bite sized pieces (about 6-7 cups of sliced leeks)

1 large onion, cut

20 black olives pitted, chopped

1/2 cup hot water

1/4 cup olive oil

1 cup rice

2 cups boiling water

black pepper, to taste

Directions:

In a large saucepan, sauté the leeks and onion in olive oil for 4-5 minutes. Cut and add the olives and 1/2 cup of water. Bring temperature down, cover saucepan, and cook for 5 minutes, stirring occasionally.

Add in rice and 2 cups of hot water, bring to a boil, cover, and simmer for 15 more minutes, stirring occasionally. Remove from heat and allow to 'sit' for 30 minutes before serving so that the rice can absorb any liquid left.

Rice and Tomato Stew

Serves: 6-7

Ingredients:

1 cup rice

1 big onion, chopped

2 cups canned tomatoes, diced or 5 big ripe tomatoes

1 tbsp paprika

1/4 cup olive oil

1 tsp savory

½ cup fresh parsley, finely cut

1 tsp sugar

Directions:

Wash and drain the rice. In a large saucepan, sauté the onion in olive oil for 4-5 minutes. Add in paprika and rice, stirring constantly, until the rice becomes transparent.

Stir in 2 cups of hot water and the tomatoes. Mix well and season with salt, pepper, savory and a tsp of sugar to neutralize the acidic taste of the tomatoes. Simmer over medium heath for about 20 minutes. When ready sprinkle with parsley.

Roasted Cauliflower

Serves: 4

Ingredients:

1 medium cauliflower, cut into florets

4 garlic cloves, lightly crushed

1 tsp fresh rosemary

salt and black pepper, to taste

1/4 cup olive oil

Directions:

Mix olive oil oil, rosemary, salt, pepper and garlic together. Toss in cauliflower and place in a baking dish in one layer.

Roast in a preheated to 350 F oven for 20 minutes; stir and bake for 10 more minutes.

New Potatoes with Herbs

Serves: 4-5

Ingredients:

2 lbs small new potatoes

5 tbsp olive oil

1 tbsp dried mint

1 tbsp finely chopped parsley

1 tbsp rosemary

1 tbsp oregano

1 tbsp dill

1 tsp salt

1 tsp black pepper

Directions:

Wash the young potatoes, cut them in halves if too big, and them in a baking dish.

Pour the olive oil over the potatoes. Season with the herbs, salt and pepper and toss to coat evenly. Bake for 30-40 minutes at 350F.

Potato and Zucchini Bake

Serves: 6

Ingredients:

1½ lb potatoes, peeled and sliced into rounds

5 zucchinis, peeled and sliced into rounds

2 onions, sliced

3 tomatoes, pureed

½ cup water

4 tbsp olive oil

1 tsp dried oregano

1/3 cup fresh parsley leaves, chopped

salt and black pepper, to taste

Directions:

Place potatoes, zucchinis and onions in a large, shallow ovenproof baking dish.

Pour over the the olive oil and pureed tomatoes. Add salt and freshly ground pepper to taste and toss the everything together. Add in water.

Bake in a preheated to 350 F oven for an hour, stirring halfway through.

Okra and Tomato Casserole

Serves: 4-5

Ingredients:

1 lb okra, stem ends trimmed

4 large tomatoes, cut into wedges

3 garlic cloves, chopped

3 tbsp olive oil

1 tsp salt

black pepper, to taste

Directions:

In a large casserole, mix together trimmed okra, sliced tomatoes, olive oil and chopped garlic. Add salt and pepper and toss to combine. Bake in a preheated to 350 F oven for 45 minutes, or until the okra is tender.

Roasted Cauliflower

Serves: 4

Ingredients:

1 medium cauliflower, cut into florets

4 garlic cloves, lightly crushed

1 tsp fresh rosemary

salt and black pepper, to taste

1/4 cup olive oil

Directions:

Mix olive oil oil, rosemary, salt, pepper and garlic together. Toss in cauliflower and place in a baking dish in one layer.

Roast in a preheated to 350 F oven for 20 minutes; stir and bake for 10 more minutes.

Roasted Brussels Sprouts

Serves: 4-5

Ingredients:

1 ½ lb Brussels sprouts, rinsed

1 tbsp summer savory

3 tbsp olive oil

3 tbsp balsamic vinegar

salt and black pepper, to taste

Directions:

Preheat the oven to 400 F. Place whole sprouts in a bowl. (If they are too large-cut in half). Add olive oil, balsamic vinegar and and summer savory and toss to coat evenly.

Season with salt and pepper. Place Brussels sprouts on a baking sheet and roast for 35 minutes, stirring a couple of times, or until tender. Serve warm.

Roasted Butternut Squash

Serves: 4

Ingredients:

½ butternut squash, peeled, seeds removed, flesh chopped

2 garlic cloves, finely chopped

2 sprigs fresh rosemary, leaves only

3-4 tbsp olive oil

salt and black pepper, to taste

Directions:

Preheat the oven to 350 F. Place the butternut squash pieces onto a baking tray and scatter over the rosemary and the chopped garlic.

Drizzle with olive oil and season, to taste, with salt and freshly ground black pepper. Transfer to the oven and roast for 12-15 minutes, or until the squash is tender and golden-brown.

Roasted Artichoke Hearts

Serves: 4

Ingredients:

2 cans artichoke hearts

4 garlic cloves, quartered

2 tbsp olive oil

1 tsp summer savory

salt and pepper, to taste

2-3 tbsp lemon juice, to serve

Directions:

Preheat oven to 350 F. Drain artichoke hearts and rinse them well. Place them in a bowl and toss in garlic, savory and olive oil.

Arrange artichoke hearts in a baking dish and bake for about 45 minutes tossing a few times if desired. Season with salt and pepper, and serve with lemon juice.

Beet Fries

Serves: 4

Ingredients:

3 beets, cut in strips

3 tbsp olive oil

1 cup finely cut spring onions

2 garlic cloves, crushed

1 tsp salt

Directions:

Line a baking dish with baking paper. Wash and peel the beets then cut them in strips similar to French fries. Toss the beets with olive oil, spring onions, garlic and salt.

Arrange the beets on a prepared baking sheet and place it in a preheated to 425 F oven for 25-30 minutes, flipping halfway through.

Grilled Vegetable Skewers

Serves: 4

Ingredients:

1 red pepper

1 green pepper

3 zucchinis, halved lengthwise and sliced

3 onions, quartered

12 medium mushrooms, whole

2 garlic cloves, crushed

2 tbsp olive oil

1 tsp summer savory

1 tsp cumin

1 spring fresh rosemary, leaves only

salt and ground black pepper, to taste

Directions:

Deseed and cut the peppers into chunks. Divide between 6 skewers threading alternately with the zucchinis, onions and mushrooms. Set aside the skewers in a shallow plate.

Mix the crushed garlic with the herbs, cumin, salt, black pepper and olive oil. Roll each skewer in the mixture. Bake them on a hot barbecue or char grill, turning occasionally, until slightly charred.

Vegan Breakfasts and Desserts

Raisin Quinoa Breakfast

Serves: 2

Ingredients:

½ cup quinoa

1 cup water

1 tbsp brown sugar

1 tsp cinnamon

½ tsp vanilla

½ tsp ground flax seed

2 tbsp walnuts or almonds, chopped

2 tbsp raisins

Directions:

Rinse quinoa and drain. Place water and quinoa into a small saucepan and bring to a boil. Add cinnamon and vanilla.

Reduce heat to low and simmer for about 15 minutes stirring often. When ready, place a portion of the quinoa into a bowl, drizzle with brown sugar and top with flax seeds, raisins and crushed walnuts.

Citrus Quinoa Breakfast

Serves: 2

Ingredients:

½ cup quinoa

1 cup water

1 orange, peeled, cut into bite-sized pieces

2 tbsp blanched almonds, chopped

2 tbsp cranberries

1 tsp lemon zest

½ tsp vanilla

Directions:

Rinse quinoa and drain. Place water and quinoa into a small saucepan and bring to a boil. Add vanilla and lemon zest.

Reduce heat to low and simmer for about 15 minutes stirring often.

When ready, place a portion of the quinoa into a bowl and top with orange segments, cranberries and almonds.

Avocado and Olive Paste on Toasted Rye Bread

Serves: 4

Ingredients:

1 avocado, peeled and finely chopped

2 tbsp black olive paste

1 tbsp lemon juice

Directions:

Mash avocados with a fork or potato masher until almost smooth. Add the black olive paste and lemon juice. Season with salt and pepper to taste. Stir to combine.

Toast 4 slices of rye bread until golden. Spoon 1/4 of the avocado mixture onto each slice of bread.

Avocado, Lettuce and Tomato Sandwiches

Serves: 2

Ingredients:

4 slices wholewheat bread

1 tbsp vegan basil pesto

2 large leaves lettuce

1/2 tomato, thinly sliced

1/2 avocado, peeled and sliced

6 slices cucumber

Directions:

Spread pesto on the four slices of bread.

Layer two slices with one lettuce leaf, two slices tomato, two slices avocado and three slices cucumber.

Top with remaining bread slices. Cut sandwiches in half and serve.

Avocado and Chickpea Sandwiches

Serves: 4

4 slices rye bread

1/2 can chickpeas, drained

1 avocado

2-3 green onions, finely chopped

1/2 tomato, thinly sliced

1/3 tsp cumin

salt, to taste

Directions:

Mash the avocado and chickpeas with a fork or potato masher until smooth. Add in green onions, cumin and salt and combine well.

Spread this mixture on the four slices of bread. Top each slice with tomato and serve.

Winter Greens Smoothie

Serves: 2

Ingredients:

2 broccoli florets, frozen

1½ cup coconut water

½ banana

½ cup pineapple

1 cup fresh spinach

2 kale leaves

Directions:

Combine ingredients in blender and blend until smooth. Enjoy!

Delicious Kale Smoothie

Serves: 2

Ingredients:

2-3 ice cubes

1½ cup apple juice

3-4 kale leaves

1 apple, cut

1 cup strawberries

½ tsp cloves

Directions:

Combine ingredients in blender and purée until smooth.

Cherry Smoothie

Serves: 2

Ingredients:

2-3 ice cubes

1½ cup almond or coconut milk

1½ cup pitted and frozen cherries

½ avocado

1 tsp cinnamon

1 tsp chia seeds

Directions:

Combine all ingredients into a blender and process until smooth. Enjoy!

Banana and Coconut Smoothie

Serves: 2

Ingredients:

1 frozen banana, chopped

1½ cup coconut water

2-3 small broccoli florets

1 tbsp coconut butter

Directions:

Add all ingredients into a blender and blend until the smoothie turns into an even and smooth consistency. Enjoy!

Vegan Walnut Pie

Serves: 15

Ingredients:

14 oz filo pastry

1 cup ground walnuts

2/3 cup vegan margarine, melted, or sunflower oil

For the syrup:

2 cups sugar

2 cups water

1 tbsp vanilla powder

2 tbsp lemon zest

Directions:

Grease a baking tray and place 2-3 sheets of pastry. Crush the walnuts and spread some evenly on the pastry. Place two more sheets of the filo pastry on top. Repeat until all the pastry sheets and walnuts have been used up. Always finish with some sheets of pastry on top. Cut the pie in the tray into small squares. Melt the margarine and pour it over the pie. Bake in a preheated oven at 350 F until light brown. When ready set aside to cool.

the syrup: Combine water and sugar in a saucepan. Add vanilla and lemon zest and bring to the boil, then lower the heat and simmer for about 5 minutes until the syrup is nearly thick. Pour hot syrup over the cold baked pie, leave to stand for at least 1-2 days until completely dry.

Baked Apples

Serves: 4

Ingredients:

8 medium sized apples

1/3 cup walnuts, crushed

3/4 cup sugar

3 tbsp raisins, soaked

vanilla, cinnamon according to taste

Directions:

Peel and carefully hollow the apples. Prepare the stuffing by mixing 3/4 cup of sugar, crushed walnuts, raisins and cinnamon.

Stuff the apples and place in an oiled dish, pour over 1-2 tbsp of water and bake in a moderate oven. Serve warm.

Apple Cake

Serves: 12

Ingredients:

4-5 medium apples, sliced, cooked and mashed

1 cup walnuts, chopped

1/2 cup apple cider

1/2 cup sunflower oil

3 1/2 cups flour

1 1/2 cups sugar

1 tbsp baking powder

1/2 tsp baking soda

a pinch of salt

1 tsp cinnamon

1 /2 tsp fresh ground cardamom

1/2 tsp ground cloves

Directions:

Combine flour, baking powder, baking soda and salt. In another bowl, mix sugar, vegetable oil and apple cider, until well blended. Add in spices and stir again.

In a smaller bowl, mash cooked apples. Add apples to liquid ingredients and mix well. Add dry ingredients to wet ingredients, stirring. Add walnuts and combine everything well.

Spread batter evenly in a lined 9×13″ baking pan. Bake in a preheated to 350 F oven for 40 minutes. When completely cooled, dust with powdered sugar and cut.

Pumpkin Baked with Dry Fruit

Serves: 5-6

Ingredients:

1.5 lb pumpkin, cut into medium pieces

1 cup dry fruit (apricots, plums, apples, raisins)

1/2 cup brown sugar

Directions:

Soak the dry fruit in some water, drain and discard the water. Cut the pumpkin in medium cubes. At the bottom of a pot arrange a layer of pumpkin pieces, then a layer of dry fruit and then again some pumpkin.

Add a little water. Cover the pot and bring to boil. Simmer until there is no more water left.

When almost ready add the sugar. Serve warm or cold.

Pumpkin Pastry

Serves: 8

Ingredients:

14 oz filo pastry

14 oz pumpkin

1 cup walnuts, coarsely chopped

1/2 cup sugar

6 tbsp sunflower oil

1 tbsp cinnamon

1 tsp vanilla

1/3 cup powdered sugar

Directions:

Grate the pumpkin and steam it until tender. Cool and add the walnuts, sugar, cinnamon and vanilla.

Place a few sheets of pastry in the baking dish, sprinkle with oil and spread the filling on top. Repeat this a few times finishing with a sheet of pastry. Bake for 20 minutes at medium heat. Let the Pumpkin Pie cool down and dust with the powdered sugar.

Apple Pastry

Serves: 8

Ingredients:

14 filo pastry

5-6 apples, peeled and cut

11/2 cup walnuts, coarsely chopped

2/3 cup sugar

6 tbsp oil

1 tbsp cinnamon

1/2 tsp vanilla extract

1/3 cup powdered sugar

Directions:

Cut the apples in small pieces and mix with the walnuts, sugar, cinnamon and vanilla. Place two sheets of pastry in the baking dish, sprinkle with oil and spread the filling on top.

Repeat this a few times finishing with a sheet of pastry. Bake for 20 minutes at medium heat.

Let the Apple Pastry cool down and dust with the powdered sugar.

Pumpkin Cake

Serves: 12

Ingredients:

2 cups grated pumpkin

11/2 cup sugar

1 tsp cinnamon

1/2 cup sunflower oil

1 cup warm water

1 cup ground walnuts

3 cups plain flour

1 tbsp baking powder

1/3 cup powdered sugar

Directions:

Combine sugar and grated pumpkin with cinnamon and leave for 15 minutes to absorb the aroma. Add oil and mix well with a fork.

Add warm water and the crushed walnuts stirring well. Mix well the baking powder with the flour and gently add to the dough.

Preheat oven to 350 F. Pour the dough in an oiled and floured 9×13″ baking pan. Bake for about 35 minutes. When ready and cold turn over a plate and sprinkle with powdered sugar.

Granny's Vegan Cake

Serves: 12

Ingredients:

1/2 cup sugar

1 cup fruit jam

1 cup cool water

1/2 cup vegetable oil

1 cup crushed walnuts

1 tsp baking soda

21/2 cups flour

1 tsp vanilla powder

½ tsp cinnamon

Directions:

Combine the baking soda with the jam and leave for 10 min. Add sugar, water, oil, walnuts and flour in that order.

Mix well and pour in a round 10 x 2-inches cake pan. Bake in a preheated to 350 F oven.

When ready turn over a plate and sprinkle with powdered sugar.

FREE BONUS RECIPES: 10 Ridiculously Easy Jam and Jelly Recipes Anyone Can Make

A Different Strawberry Jam

Makes 6-7 11 oz jars

Ingredients:

4 lb fresh small strawberries (stemmed and cleaned)

5 cups sugar

1 cup water

2 tbsp lemon juice or 1 tsp citric acid

Directions:

Mix water and sugar and bring to the boil. Simmer sugar syrup for 5-6 minutes then slowly drop in the cleaned strawberries. Stir and bring to the boil again. Lower heat and simmer, stirring and skimming any foam off the top once or twice.

Drop a small amount of the jam on a plate and wait a minute to see if it has thickened. If it has gelled enough, turn off the heat. If not, keep boiling and test every 5 minutes until ready. Two or three minutes before you remove the jam from the heat, add lemon juice or citric acid and stir well.

Ladle the hot jam in the jars until 1/8-inch from the top. Place the lid on top and flip the jar upside down. Continue until all of the jars are filled and upside down. Allow the jam to cool completely before turning right-side up.

Press on the lid to check and see if it has sealed. If one of the jars lids doesn't pop up- the jar is not sealed–store it in a refrigerator.

Raspberry Jam

Makes 4-5 11 oz jars

Ingredients:

4 cups raspberries

4 cups sugar

1 tsp vanilla extract

1/2 tsp citric acid

Directions:

Gently wash and drain the raspberries. Lightly crush them with a potato masher, food mill or a food processor. Do not puree, it is better to have bits of fruit. Sieve half of the raspberry pulp to remove some of the seeds.

Combine sugar and raspberries in a wide, thick-bottomed pot and bring mixture to a full rolling boil, stirring constantly. Skim any scum or foam that rises to the surface. Boil until the jam sets.

Test by putting a small drop on a cold plate – if the jam is set, it will wrinkle when given a small poke with your finger. Add citric acid, vanilla, and stir. Simmer for 2-3 minutes more, then ladle into hot jars. Flip upside down or process 10 minutes in boiling water.

Raspberry-Peach Jam

Makes 4-5 11 oz jars

Ingredients:

2 lb peaches

1 1/2 cup raspberries

4 cups sugar

1 tsp citric acid

Directions:

Wash and slice the peaches. Clean the raspberries and combine them with the peaches is a wide, heavy-bottomed saucepan. Cover with sugar and set aside for a few hours or overnight. Bring the fruit and sugar to a boil over medium heat, stirring occasionally. Remove any foam that rises to the surface.

Boil until the jam sets. Add citric acid and stir. Simmer for 2-3 minutes more, then ladle into hot jars. Flip upside down or process 10 minutes in boiling water.

Blueberry Jam

Makes 4-5 11 oz jars

Ingredients:

4 cups granulated sugar

3 cups blueberries (frozen and thawed or fresh)

3/4 cup honey

2 tbsp lemon juice

1 tsp lemon zest

Directions:

Gently wash and drain the blueberries. Lightly crush them with a potato masher, food mill or a food processor. Add the honey, lemon juice, and lemon zest, then bring to a boil over medium-high heat. Boils for 10-15 minutes, stirring from time to time. Boil until the jam sets.

Test by putting a small drop on a cold plate – if the jam is set, it will wrinkle when given a small poke with your finger. Skim off any foam, then ladle the jam into jars. Seal, flip upside down or process for 10 minutes in boiling water.

Triple Berry Jam

Makes 4-5 11 oz jars

Ingredients:

1 cup strawberries

1 cup raspberries

2 cups blueberries

4 cups sugar

1 tsp citric acid

Directions:

Mix berries and add sugar. Set aside for a few hours or overnight. Bring the fruit and sugar to the boil over medium heat, stirring frequently. Remove any foam that rises to the surface. Boil until the jam sets. Add citric acid, salt and stir.

Simmer for 2-3 minutes more, then ladle into hot jars. Flip upside down or process 10 minutes in boiling water.

Red Currant Jelly

Makes 6-7 11 oz jars

Ingredients:

2 lb fresh red currants

1/2 cup water

3 cups sugar

1 tsp citric acid

Directions:

Place the currants into a large pot, and crush with a potato masher or berry crusher. Add in water, and bring to a boil. Simmer for 10 minutes. Strain the fruit through a jelly or cheese cloth and measure out 4 cups of the juice. Pour the juice into a large saucepan, and stir in the sugar.

Bring to full rolling boil, then simmer for 20-30 minutes, removing any foam that may rise to the surface. When the jelly sets, ladle in hot jars, flip upside down or process in boiling water for 10 minutes.

White Cherry Jam

Makes 3-4 11 oz jars

Ingredients:

2 lb cherries

3 cups sugar

2 cups water

1 tsp citric acid

Directions:

Wash and stone cherries. Combine water and sugar and bring to the boil. Boil for 5-6 minutes then remove from heat and add cherries.

Bring to a rolling boil and cook until set. Add citric acid, stir and boil 1-2 minutes more.

Ladle in hot jars, flip upside down or process in boiling water for 10 minutes.

Cherry Jam

Makes 3-4 11 oz jars

Ingredients:

2 lb fresh cherries, pitted, halved

4 cups sugar

1/2 cup lemon juice

Directions:

Place the cherries in a large saucepan. Add sugar and set aside for an hour. Add the lemon juice and place over low heat.

Cook, stirring occasionally, for 10 minutes or until sugar dissolves. Increase heat to high and bring to a rolling boil.

Cook for 5-6 minutes or until jam is set. Remove from heat and ladle hot jam into jars, seal and flip upside down.

Oven Baked Ripe Figs Jam

Makes 3-4 11 oz jars

Ingredients:

2 lb ripe figs

2 cups sugar

1 ½ cups water

2 tbsp lemon juice

Directions:

Arrange the figs in a Dutch oven, if they are very big, cut them in halves. Add sugar and water and stir well. Bake at 350 F for about one and a half hours. Do not stir.

You can check the readiness by dropping a drop of the syrup in a cup of cold water – if it falls to the bottom without dissolving, the jam is ready. If the drop dissolves before falling, you can bake it a little longer.

Take out of the oven, add lemon juice and ladle in the warm jars. Place the lids on top and flip the jars upside down. Allow the jam to cool completely before turning right-side up.

If you want to process the jams - place them into a large pot, cover the jars with water by at least 2 inches and bring to a boil. Boil for 10 minutes, remove the jars and sit to cool.

Quince Jam

Makes 5-6 11 oz jars

Ingredients:

4 lb quinces

5 cups sugar

2 cups water

1 tsp lemon zest

3 tbsp lemon juice

Directions:

Combine water and sugar in a deep, thick-bottomed saucepan and bring it to the boil. Simmer, stirring until the sugar has completely dissolved. Rinse the quinces, cut in half, and discard the cores.

Grate the quinces, using a cheese grater or a blender to make it faster. Quince flesh tends to darken very quickly, so it is good to do this as fast as possible. Add the grated quinces to the sugar syrup and cook uncovered, stirring occasionally until the jam turns pink and thickens to desired consistency, about 40 minutes.

Drop a small amount of the jam on a plate and wait a minute to see if it has thickened. If it has gelled enough, turn off the heat. If not, keep boiling and test every 2-3 minutes until ready.

Two or three minutes before you remove the jam from the heat, add lemon juice and lemon zest and stir well.

Ladle in hot, sterilized jars and flip upside down.

About the Author

Vesela lives in Bulgaria with her family of six (including the Jack Russell Terrier). Her passion is going green in everyday life and she loves to prepare homemade cosmetic and beauty products for all her family and friends.

Vesela has been publishing her cookbooks for over a year now. If you want to see other healthy family recipes that she has published, together with some natural beauty books, you can check out her Author Page on Amazon.